The Usborne Story of Art Picture Book

Sarah Courtauld

Illustrated by Karine Bernadou   Designed by Nicola Butler

Edited by Jane Chisholm and Rosie Dickins

Expert advice by Kathleen Adler

CONTENTS

		Drama	13			
The first artists	2	In the north	14	Bright and bold	24
The Middle Ages	4	Frocks and frills	16	Wild and free	26
Colourful crowds	6	Peace	18	Breaking the rules	27
Down to earth	7	War	19	Shapes and dreams	28
Gods and monsters	8	Landscape	20	Think again	29
Bigger and better	10	Legends	21	Timeline	30
Powerful portraits	12	Making an impression	22	Index	32

THE FIRST ARTISTS

Thousands and thousands of years ago, long before writing was invented, people painted pictures. Some people believed that these pictures had magical powers.

Around 17,000 years ago, people used small pieces of chalk and earth to draw these animals on the walls of caves.

BISON
Painted around 17,000 years ago in Lascaux, France

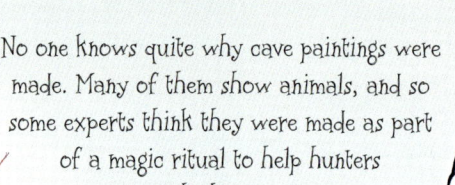

HORSE
Painted around 17,000 years ago in Lascaux, France

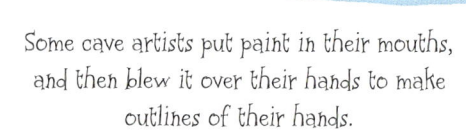

No one knows quite why cave paintings were made. Many of them show animals, and so some experts think they were made as part of a magic ritual to help hunters catch their prey.

Some cave artists put paint in their mouths, and then blew it over their hands to make outlines of their hands.

Around 3,500 years ago, ancient Egyptians were making elaborate paintings on the walls of tombs. They believed in life after death, and they painted things that they hoped people would be able to enjoy after they had died.

The painting comes from the tomb of a rich man called Nebamun, and shows his garden. The trees are brimming with delicious fruit.

ORNAMENTAL POOL FROM THE TOMB OF NEBAMUN
Painted about 3,360 years ago in Egypt

The pond is full of ducks and fish for Nebamun to catch and eat.

2

17,000–2,000 years ago

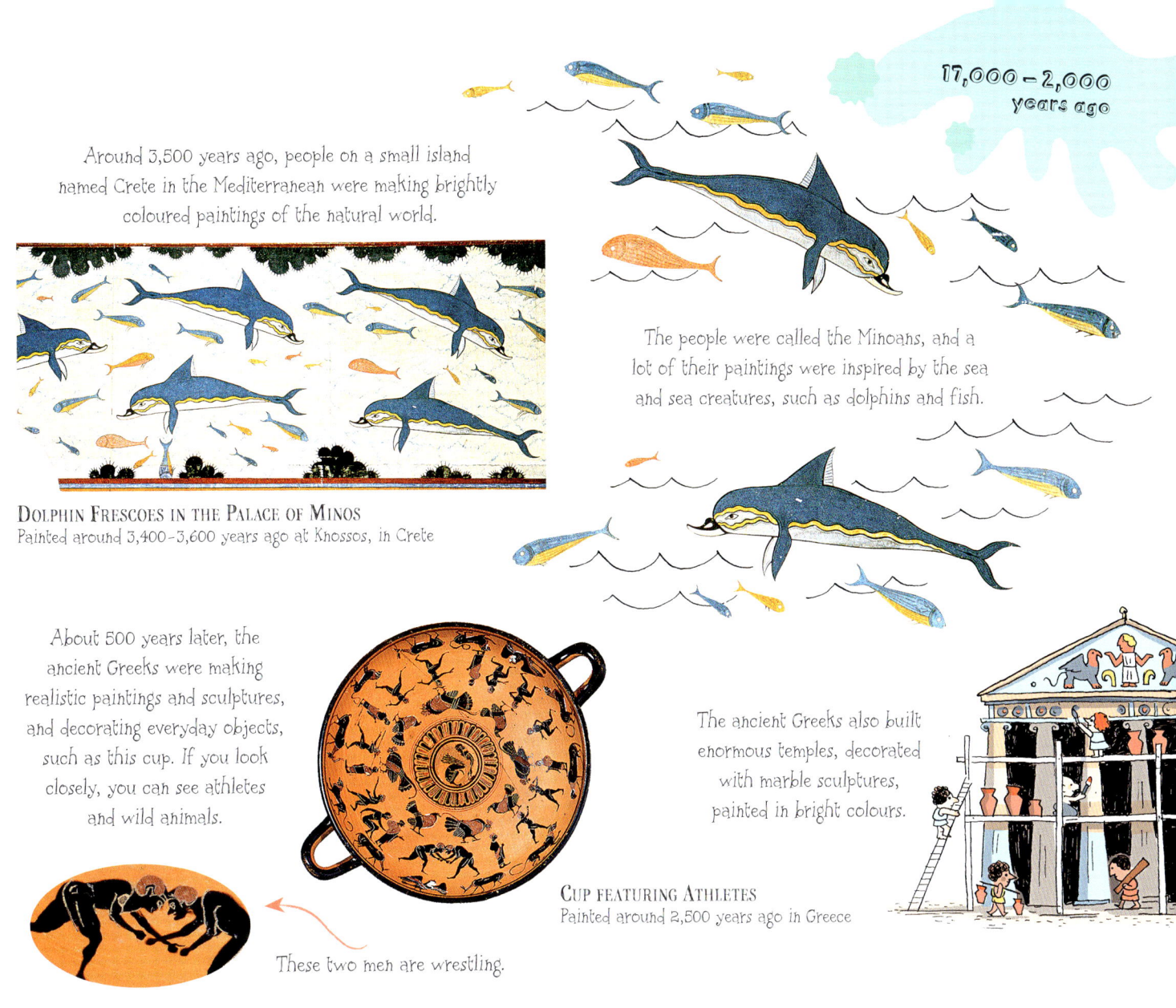

Around 3,500 years ago, people on a small island named Crete in the Mediterranean were making brightly coloured paintings of the natural world.

DOLPHIN FRESCOES IN THE PALACE OF MINOS
Painted around 3,400–3,600 years ago at Knossos, in Crete

The people were called the Minoans, and a lot of their paintings were inspired by the sea and sea creatures, such as dolphins and fish.

About 500 years later, the ancient Greeks were making realistic paintings and sculptures, and decorating everyday objects, such as this cup. If you look closely, you can see athletes and wild animals.

These two men are wrestling.

CUP FEATURING ATHLETES
Painted around 2,500 years ago in Greece

The ancient Greeks also built enormous temples, decorated with marble sculptures, painted in bright colours.

This ancient Greek sculpture of a horse's head comes from a huge temple, and would originally have been painted.

It was once part of a larger sculpture. The horse was speeding across the sky pulling a chariot. That's why its eyes are bulging and its mouth is gaping.

HEAD OF A HORSE OF SELENE, FROM THE PARTHENON
Sculpted around 2,450 years ago in Greece

The ancient Romans were inspired by the ancient Greeks to create lifelike works of art. This ancient Roman painting of birds was used as a sign for a café.

SIGN FOR A THERMOPOLIUM
Painted about 2,000 years ago in Italy

3

THE MIDDLE AGES

By the 5th century, Christianity was spreading through Europe, and many artists began to make dazzling works of religious art. They filled books with detailed illustrations, and painted glowing pictures for churches.

Printing hadn't been invented, so monks and nuns spent hours and hours copying out handmade books, and adding illustrations. One book could take years to finish.

Old book for copying

Newly copied page

CHRIST ENTHRONED FROM THE BOOK OF KELLS
Painted around 700 to 800

This is a page from *The Book of Kells*, a book of Bible stories made by monks in the 8th or 9th century.

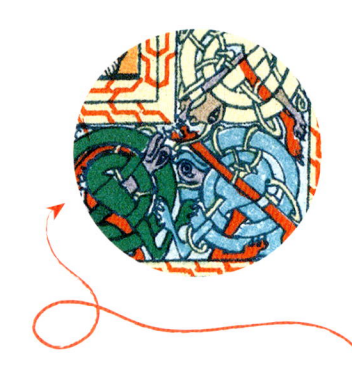

The border shows snakes curling around each other.

This illustration of a Bible story shows an angel soaring over a burning city.

The paint was made from eggs mixed with coloured powders, known as pigments, to make the different colours. Pigments came from all sorts of different things.

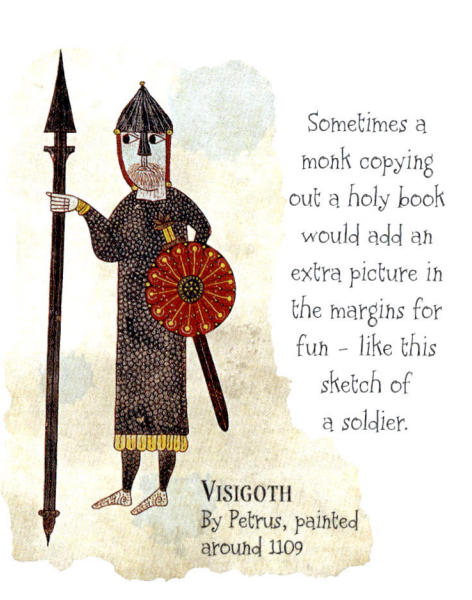

THE BURNING OF BABYLON
Painted around 1200-1300

Sometimes a monk copying out a holy book would add an extra picture in the margins for fun — like this sketch of a soldier.

VISIGOTH
By Petrus, painted around 1109

For example, beetles were crushed to make red pigment.

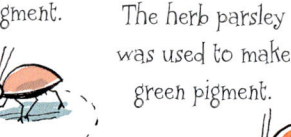

The herb parsley was used to make green pigment.

4

From 475-1430

Churches were decorated with pictures of Bible stories, to help explain the stories to people who couldn't read. This painting tells a story about the Virgin Mary.

The golden background is made with real gold, hammered into thin sheets called gold leaf.

An angel visits Mary and tells her that she's going to have a child. There are words coming out of the angel's mouth, engraved into the gold leaf...

THE ANNUNCIATION
By Simone Martini and Lippo Memmi, dated 1333

...it's a bit like a speech bubble in a cartoon.

This detail shows the holy spirit in the form of a dove.

In the Middle Ages, successful artists had busy workshops with lots of assistants to help them. One of the most important tasks in the workshop was preparing the pigments.

Assistants would learn by copying the style of the master painter.

Some artists made pictures, called mosaics, from small pieces of coloured stone or glass.

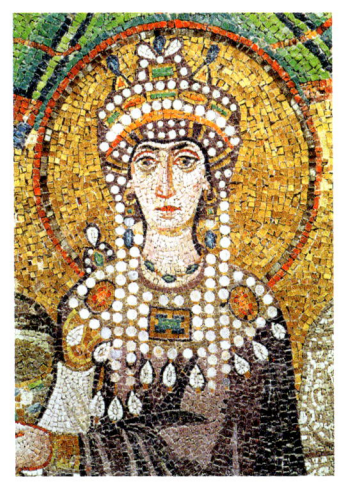

In Russia, artists painted pictures of saints on wood, which were called icons.

At the time, many people believed that paintings were holy. Some people even thought this painting of the Virgin Mary and Jesus had miraculous powers.

MADONNA AND CHILD
Painted around 1370-1430

This mosaic shows a saint and leader named Empress Theodora, who ruled over the Byzantine empire, a vast empire in Eastern Europe.

Lots of Byzantine churches were covered in glittering mosaics such as this one.

EMPRESS THEODORA
Made around 528

5

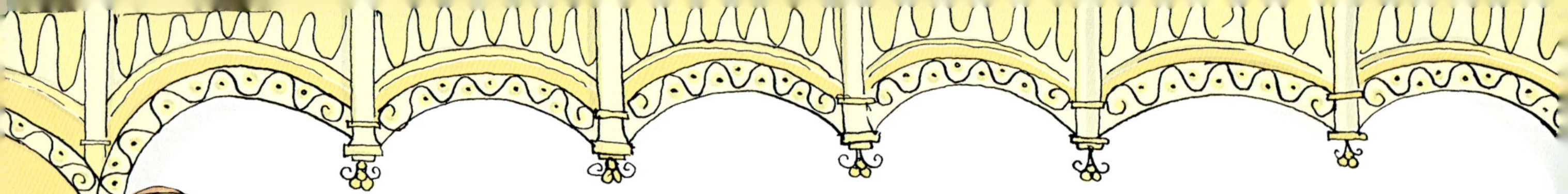

COLOURFUL CROWDS

In central Europe in the 15th century, it became fashionable for rich people to buy grand works of art. Lots of artists started painting very ornate, elegant pictures.

From 1400-1430

This painting shows the journey of the three wise men to visit the baby Jesus.

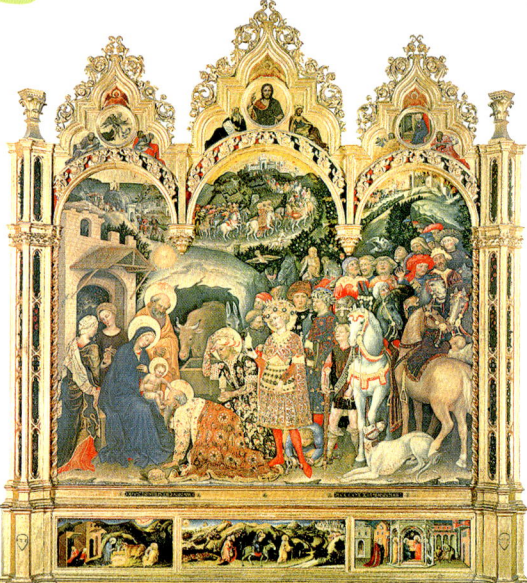

There are lots of animals and birds in the painting. Look out for...

A cheetah

A camel and a pair of monkeys

A lion

A falcon

This tall, graceful figure is one of the wise men. Notice how detailed his costume is.

ADORATION OF THE MAGI
By Gentile da Fabriano, dated 1423

This incredibly detailed painting of a feast comes from an illustrated book. It was made by three artist brothers, Herman, Paul and Jean Limbourg, for a very wealthy Duke.

The Duke is enjoying his feast...

...and so are his little dogs.

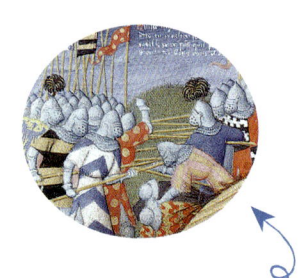

In a tapestry on the wall, knights are fighting.

The sky shows the constellations visible in January.

JANUARY, FROM THE VERY RICH HOURS OF THE DUKE OF BERRY
By the Limbourg Brothers, begun around 1410

6

DOWN TO EARTH

From 1430–1500

While artists in central Europe created elaborate, golden scenes, in northern Europe, many artists painted more everyday subjects, in a simpler style.

In the Netherlands, an artist called Jan van Eyck used a new technique known as oil painting to make this lifelike portrait of a couple in their home. The painting is full of details to spot. Look out for...

Two pairs of shoes. Both the man and the woman have taken off their outdoor shoes.

Oranges. These show off the couple's wealth, as oranges were a luxury at the time.

A mirror. If you look very closely, you can see the couple reflected in it.

THE ARNOLFINI PORTRAIT
By Jan van Eyck, painted in 1434

While lots of artists painted realistic scenes, artist Hieronymus Bosch has added bizarre imaginary creatures to this oil painting, to help illustrate a story about greed.

To make an oil painting, artists mixed their pigments with oil. Then they painted the picture in lots of thin, semi-see-through layers.

Oil

Pigment

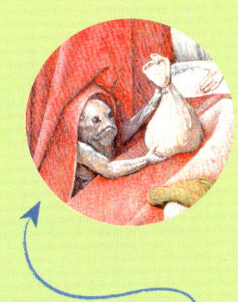

A devil is offering a greedy man the chance to sell his soul for a sack of money. But the figure of death is already knocking at the door.

Look out for other supernatural creatures in the room.

PORTRAIT OF A LADY
Workshop of Rogier van der Weyden, painted around 1460

Oil paint was very good for showing different textures. Notice how amazingly lifelike this woman's veil looks.

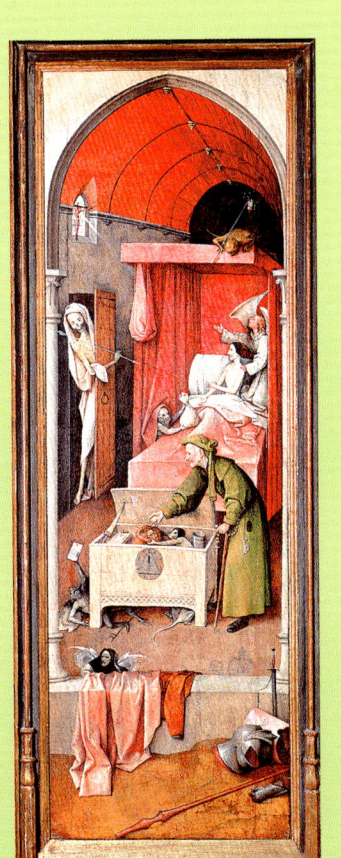

DEATH AND THE MISER
By Hieronymus Bosch, painted around 1485–90

GODS AND MONSTERS

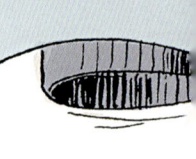

In the 15th century in Italy, many painters began to be inspired by the art and stories of ancient Rome and Greece. They wanted their paintings to look as lifelike as ancient Greek and Roman sculptures.

The period between the 15th and the 17th centuries in Italy became known as the 'Renaissance', which means 'rebirth'. People rediscovered lots of painting skills that had been forgotten since ancient Greek and Roman times.

A monk, Fra Filippo Lippi, made this elegant painting of the Angel Gabriel visiting the Virgin Mary.

THE ANNUNCIATION
By Fra Filippo Lippi, painted in 1450-3

Notice how real the faces in the painting look - Filippo Lippi made lots of sketches from life, and was famous for his simple, natural style.

Look out for the roses floating through the air. According to the myth, roses appeared when Venus was born.

This painting was based on an ancient Roman myth. It shows the birth of Venus, goddess of beauty, as she springs out of a shell in the ocean.

This is a wind God, Zephyrus, with a goddess of the breeze, Aura. Together, they blow Venus to the shore.

The artist based the figure of Venus on an ancient Roman statue.

THE BIRTH OF VENUS
By Sandro Botticelli, painted around 1485

8

From 1450-1513

This dramatic painting celebrates a battle between Florence and Siena, two cities in Italy. The central figure is the leader of the victorious Florentine army.

THE BATTLE OF SAN ROMANO
By Paolo Uccello, painted around 1438-40

The artist was so fond of painting animals and birds that he became known by the nickname, 'Paulo Uccello', which means 'Paul of the birds'.

Uccello drew his horses from a small wooden model. That's why they all look so similar.

Uccello collected paintings of birds and animals.

This painting combines several scenes from a famous ancient Greek myth.

1
Princess Andromeda is chained to a rock, and is about to be eaten by a sea monster. A hero named Perseus flies in to save her, using his magical winged sandals.

PERSEUS FREES ANDROMEDA
By Piero di Cosimo, painted around 1513

2
Perseus kills the monster.

3
Perseus and Andromeda fall in love and get married.

9

BIGGER AND BETTER

The next generation of Italian artists wanted their paintings to look even more lifelike than the last. The most successful artists became very famous and took on grand projects...

A brilliant artist from Florence, called Michelangelo, painted the entire ceiling of the Sistine Chapel, an enormous chapel in Rome, with religious scenes. Michelangelo wanted the figures in his paintings to look very real. He even looked at dead bodies to help him draw human bodies more accurately.

Here, God is about to create Adam, the first man on Earth.

SCENES FROM THE SISTINE CHAPEL CEILING
By Michelangelo, painted between 1508 and 1512

In this scene, God creates the sun.

This woman is the Delphic Sibyl, a prophetess from ancient Greece, who some people believe predicted the birth of Jesus.

This detail shows the hand of God, reaching out to give life to Adam.

"My brush is always above me, its drips and dribbles making a splendid mosaic on my face below!"
Michelangelo

It took Michelangelo four years to complete the ceiling. He wouldn't let anyone see it until it was finished, and he was furious with the Pope when he sneaked a look.

From 1490

This painting is by Leonardo da Vinci, another great artist from Florence. It shows Mary with Jesus, John the Baptist and an angel.

Notice the soft shadows that Leonardo has added to the angel's face. He wanted the painting to look as if it was being seen through a veil of smoke.

The Virgin of the Rocks
By Leonardo da Vinci, painted in about 1491-1508

Before starting to paint, Leonardo made a drawing. He pricked tiny holes in it, laid it over a wooden panel, and rubbed charcoal over it.

When he took the paper away, an outline was left on the surface underneath.

There are two different drawings hidden under the surface of *The Virgin of the Rocks*. Leonardo started drawing the design for a completely different painting, and then changed his mind.

This scene shows a moment from a Greek myth, when a god called Bacchus (wearing a pink cloak) sees a woman called Ariadne, and falls in love with her.

Bacchus and Ariadne was made for a wealthy Duke who kept lots of animals, including cheetahs. These cheetahs were probably based on the Duke's pets.

Notice how bright the colours are in the painting. The artist, Titian, was known for using rich, beautiful colours.

Bacchus and Ariadne
By Titian, painted in 1520-3

The dragon has broken St. George's lance - you can see the end sticking out of its chest.

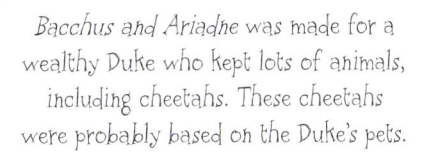

This dramatic painting illustrates the legend of St. George and the Dragon. St. George rescues a princess from a dragon who was about to eat her.

In the background, the rescued princess is running away.

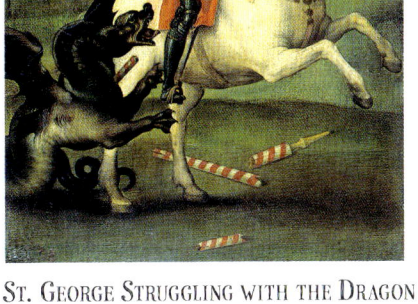

St. George Struggling with the Dragon
By Raphael, painted around 1506

11

1500s–1600s

POWERFUL PORTRAITS

In the 16th century, some brilliant artists made their living by painting portraits of wealthy and important people.

This double portrait shows two friends, Jean de Dinteville (on the left) and Georges de Selve (on the right), surrounded by objects which show how wealthy, cultured and well-travelled they are. Look out for...

A case of flutes and two lutes

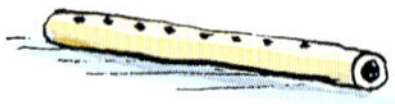

A portable sundial, which was used on ships for navigation

A gold dagger

A globe showing the stars

The strange object on the floor is actually a distorted skull. You can only see it clearly if you look at it from the side – close one eye and look along the line of the arrows.

THE AMBASSADORS
By Hans Holbein the Younger, painted in 1533

The artist probably added the skull as a reminder that everyone dies, no matter how wealthy or important they are.

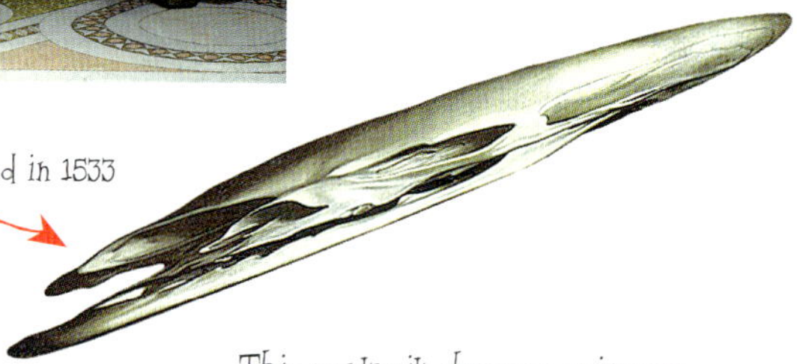

This portrait shows a princess named Margarita. She was the favourite daughter of a Spanish king.

This unusual portrait of a king is made up of flowers, fruit and vegetables.

It was painted by Arcimboldo for King Rudolf II of Austria. As well as painting portraits, Arcimboldo also designed costumes for plays at Rudolf's court.

In one of them, when Rudolf was only six, Arcimboldo played a giant – and Rudolf played a brave dwarf.

PORTRAIT OF RUDOLF II
By Giuseppe Arcimboldo, painted in about 1590

PORTRAIT OF THE INFANTA MARGARITA IN A PINK DRESS
By Juan Bautista Martínez del Mazo, painted around 1665

12

From 1550

DRAMA

At around the same time, other artists started working in a theatrical new style, painting dramatic moments or scenes from scary stories.

All the paintings on this page use bright light and dark backgrounds. This gives the paintings a more dramatic atmosphere.

In this painting by Caravaggio, a boy leaps back in fright because a lizard has just bitten his finger.

This painting by Rembrandt shows a scene from a Bible story about a king named Belshazzar. After he steals a sacred cup, a message appears on the wall, telling him his days are numbered. Belshazzar dies that very night.

BOY BITTEN BY A LIZARD
By Caravaggio, painted about 1594-5

Caravaggio and Rembrandt were both fascinated by how people's faces show their feelings. Rembrandt pulled faces in a mirror to help him draw different facial expressions.

BELSHAZZAR'S FEAST
By Rembrandt, painted in about 1636-8

The woman in the red dress is so shocked, she's spilling wine out of her golden cup.

This scene shows a moment from a grisly Bible story. A woman named Judith has just cut off the head of her enemy, and her servant is holding it.

JUDITH AND MAIDSERVANT WITH THE HEAD OF HOLOFERNES
By Artemisia Gentileschi, painted in about 1623-5

Judith looks up nervously, as if she's scared of getting caught.

Belshazzar's eyes are bulging with fear.

IN THE NORTH

By the 16th century, painters in the Netherlands were making incredibly vivid paintings inspired by everyday life.

Children are playing more than 80 different games in this painting by the artist Bruegel.

There are children standing on their heads...

playing leapfrog...

...and climbing on a wooden bar. See how many other games you can spot.

CHILDREN'S GAMES
By Pieter Bruegel the Elder, painted in 1560

The busy scene on the right shows children misbehaving while their mother is asleep. Look for the child stealing the purse and the children giving the family's food to the cat.

This peaceful scene shows a girl playing a virginal - a type of keyboard popular at the time.

THE EFFECTS OF INTEMPERANCE
By Jan Steen, painted in about 1663-5

Notice all the different textures in this painting - Vermeer was known for his amazing skill at painting different materials.

Vermeer painted the girl's sleeve with a colour called lead white. No one realized it at the time, but lead white was extremely poisonous. Several artists who used lead white complained it made them feel sick.

A YOUNG WOMAN SEATED AT A VIRGINAL
By Johannes Vermeer, painted in about 1670-2

1550s-1600s

This highly detailed painting shows a bright bouquet of flowers, including several tulips. There are also bugs hidden among the flowers. Look out for...

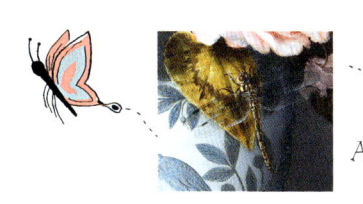

A butterfly

A dragonfly

A fly

A caterpillar

A bumblebee

A STILL LIFE OF FLOWERS IN A WAN-LI VASE
By Ambrosius Bosschaert the Elder, painted in 1609-10

At the time, paintings of flowers were very popular, as people in the Netherlands were obsessed with rare tulips. In 1636, one extremely rare tulip bulb was apparently sold in exchange for four cows, eight pigs, twelve sheep, two bottles of wine, four barrels of beer, a suit of clothes, a thousand pounds (450kg) of cheese and a silver cup.

This busy winter scene is full of details to spot. There are people playing golf, carriages rattling along and skaters whizzing across the ice.

A couple are dressed in their finest clothes.

A SCENE ON THE ICE NEAR A TOWN
By Hendrick Avercamp, painted in about 1615

A woman has just fallen over.

A man is pulling two children along in a sledge.

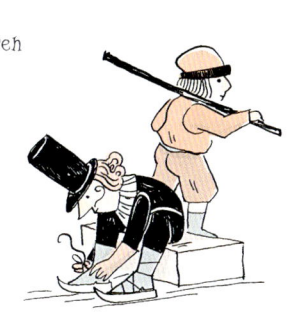

15

FROCKS AND FRILLS

By the 18th century, a delicate, pretty style had come into fashion. Artists painted portraits of wealthy people in extravagant outfits.

The couple in this portrait were called William and Elizabeth Hallett. They probably had this portrait painted to celebrate their marriage.

Elizabeth is wearing an expensive dress, but she wouldn't really have worn it on a country walk. The artist, Thomas Gainsborough, painted the clothes on mannequins in his studio.

One of the paints that Gainsborough used was called mummy brown. Amazingly, it was made by crushing up Egyptian mummies.

The painting may have been made as a sign for a café.

This painting shows a pantomime character named Pierrot. A sad clown, Pierrot was always getting his heart broken.

MR AND MRS WILLIAM HALLETT (THE MORNING WALK)
By Thomas Gainsborough, painted in 1785

PIERROT, FORMERLY KNOWN AS GILLES
By Jean-Antoine Watteau, painted around 1718-19

A Spanish artist named Goya painted this young son of a count, dressed in a bright red outfit. He's holding a pet magpie on a string.

Goya may have painted this picture after the child died. Artists sometimes painted birds as a symbol of the human soul. It's possible that Goya added the cats staring greedily at the bird to show how fragile life can be.

The artist has added his signature on the piece of paper in the magpie's mouth.

Three cats are staring at the magpie, as if they might be about to pounce.

MANUEL OSORIO MANRIQUE DE ZUÑIGA
By Francisco de Goya, painted between 1784 and 1792

From 1700

It was fashionable to paint portraits of people in gardens or woods – this picture shows Madame de Pompadour in the garden of her countryside castle.

Madame de Pompadour was the mistress of the French King, and this portrait includes a message for him. Her fan is pointing to her pet dog – and dogs are a symbol of loyalty. She's saying to the King that she will be loyal to him.

Madame de Pompadour's dog

MADAME DE POMPADOUR
By François Boucher, painted in 1759

The French Queen, Marie Antoinette, had more than 30 portraits of herself painted by her favourite artist, Elisabeth Vigée Le Brun.

This painting shows a woman on a swing with an admirer below, gazing up at her.

This statue is of Cupid, the Roman god of love. He's put his finger to his lips, because the woman has a secret admirer.

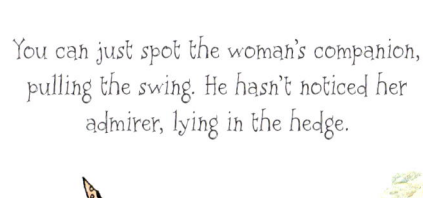

THE SWING
By Jean-Honoré Fragonard, painted in 1767

You can just spot the woman's companion, pulling the swing. He hasn't noticed her admirer, lying in the hedge.

Le Brun described how she enjoyed singing duets with the Queen as she painted her – even though Marie Antoinette sang completely out of tune.

MARIE ANTOINETTE, QUEEN OF FRANCE
By Elisabeth Louise Vigée Le Brun, painted in 1779

1648-1800s

PEACE

From the 17th century onwards, some French artists painted pictures with a very peaceful atmosphere.

French artist Claude painted lots of spacious, sunlit landscapes. This port scene is supposed to illustrate a story about an ancient queen, but she's quite hard to spot.

In fact, she's standing on the steps, about to set off on a sea voyage. Since Claude has made her so small, he was probably more interested in painting the dawn sky and the gently lapping waves.

SEAPORT WITH THE EMBARKATION OF THE QUEEN OF SHEBA
By Claude, painted in 1648

Claude completely invented the port in this painting.

The artist Ingres liked to paint people looking like perfect versions of themselves. He loved the paintings of earlier Italian artists, and copied this woman's face from a painting by the artist Raphael.

Ingres was also inspired by ancient Greek sculptures.

This boy looks totally absorbed in what he is doing – making a house of cards. The artist, Chardin, was famous for his carefully observed paintings of everyday life, which capture quiet moments.

STUDY FOR AN ODALISQUE
By Jean-Auguste-Dominique Ingres, painted in 1808

Ingres studied painting with other students at a studio in Paris.

THE HOUSE OF CARDS
By Jean-Siméon Chardin, painted in about 1736-7

18

WAR

From 1800

In the 19th century, wars broke out across Europe – and a new generation of artists painted bold scenes of soldiers and battles.

This dramatic portrait shows a famous French military leader, Napoleon, crossing the Alps to invade Italy.

NAPOLEON CROSSING THE ALPS
By Jacques-Louis David, painted around 1804

The painting was designed to flatter Napoleon, and it wasn't accurate – he actually crossed the Alps on a mule, in sunny weather.

Napoleon didn't have time to sit for the painting, so David copied the leader's head from a sculpture. And David got his own son to model the pose, perched precariously on a ladder.

This boy is holding pistols in both hands.

This painting shows an imaginary scene from a real revolution that took place in France in 1830. The woman holding the French flag is a symbol of Liberty, and she's leading her army of citizens to freedom.

LIBERTY LEADING THE PEOPLE
By Eugène Delacroix, painted in 1830

Spanish artist Goya painted the brutal side of war.

When the French army invaded Spain in 1808, hundreds of citizens fought back – and were shot by French soldiers. Goya painted this picture as a tribute to the bravery of the Spanish rebels.

THE 3RD OF MAY 1808 IN MADRID: THE EXECUTIONS ON PRINCIPE PIO HILL
By Francisco de Goya, painted in 1814

From 1817

LANDSCAPE

In the 19th century, lots of artists painted wild, lonely-looking landscapes. They went on sketching trips to the countryside to inspire them.

This blustery seascape is by English artist, J.M.W. Turner. Turner became fascinated by the sea when he was a boy. He made sketches on ships out at sea, and loved the ocean so much, he earned the nickname 'The Old Sea Captain'.

MARGATE (?) FROM THE SEA
By J.M.W. Turner, painted around 1835-40

For the time, Turner's painting methods were quite unusual. He used big, rough brushstrokes and was always experimenting with new paints. He even tried smearing tobacco on his paintings.

Notice the big, golden brushstrokes Turner has used to paint the swirling waves.

Turner was sometimes seen adding the finishing touches to his paintings when they were already hanging on gallery walls.

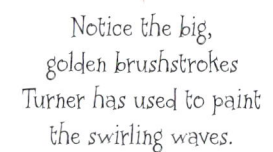

Dramatic scenes of nature were all the rage, but John Constable just liked painting places he was fond of - such as this country lane close to his childhood home.

When he was a child, Constable had walked along the lane to go to school. He probably drank from the stream, just like this little boy.

German artist Friedrich painted pictures of people alone in wild, beautiful places. This scene shows a man gazing out over foggy mountain peaks.

THE CORNFIELD
By John Constable, painted in 1826

WANDERER ABOVE THE SEA OF FOG
By Caspar David Friedrich, painted around 1817

20

LEGENDS

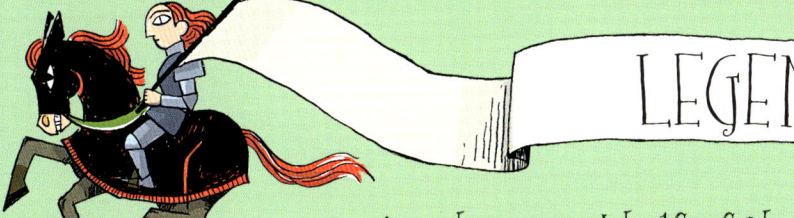

From 1870

During the second half of the 19th century, there was a fashion for imaginary scenes inspired by poems, myths and legends.

This picture is by French artist Gustave Moreau. It shows a dramatic moment from the famous legend of St. George and the dragon, as George slays the dragon with his lance.

George fought the dragon to save a princess – who you can see kneeling in the background.

ST. GEORGE AND THE DRAGON
By Gustave Moreau, painted in 1889-90

The woman in this painting was based on ancient sculptures of sleeping magical spirits from Greek myths.

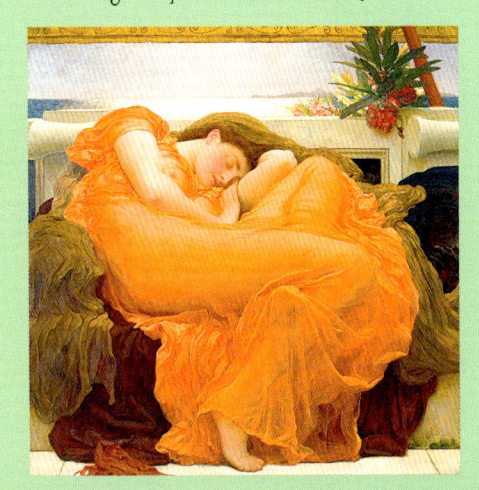

The dragon was just one of many mythical beasts Moreau painted. "I have allowed my imagination free play, and I have not been led astray by it," he said.

FLAMING JUNE
By Frederic, Lord Leighton, painted around 1895

A famous poem called 'The Lady of Shalott' inspired this scene. In the poem, the lady was trapped in a castle by an evil curse...

1 She would die if she looked out of the window, so she watched the world through a mirror.

2  When she heard a knight singing a beautiful song, she couldn't resist looking out at him.

3 Knowing the curse was going to kill her, she ran out of the tower and floated down a river in a boat, singing songs until she died.

THE LADY OF SHALOTT
By John William Waterhouse, painted in 1888

MAKING AN IMPRESSION

In the 1870s, a group of young artists in Paris started painting in a rough, sketchy style and exhibited their paintings together. They became known as the 'Impressionists'.

In the 1840s, resealable metal paint tubes were invented. This made it easier for artists to take their paintboxes and work outside.

One artist who loved painting outside was Claude-Oscar Monet.

THE WATER-LILY POND
By Claude-Oscar Monet, painted in 1899

This scene shows the pond in Monet's garden. Monet was obsessed with capturing the effects of sunlight. He painted his garden hundreds of times in different lights.

From far away, the lilies look quite lifelike...

...but close up, you can see they are just big blobs of paint.

One of Monet's paintings was called 'Sunrise: An Impression'. An art critic who saw it hated it, and wrote a rude article calling Monet an 'Impressionist'. The name stuck, and soon Monet and his friends were all known as 'Impressionists'.

Instead of blending all his colours together, Monet used dabs of pure colour.

Cézanne went on lots of walks in the countryside to paint bright, sunny landscapes like this one.

THE CHÂTEAU DE MÉDAN
By Paul Cézanne, painted around 1880

AT THE THEATRE
By Mary Cassatt, drawn around 1879
The Nelson-Atkins Museum of Art, Kansas City, Missouri

This sketchy pastel drawing by Mary Cassatt shows her sister, Lydia, at the opera.

Cassatt's parents disapproved of her becoming an artist. At the time, art wasn't seen as a respectable profession for a woman. But Cassatt decided to become an artist anyway – and was a great success.

From 1870

This pastel drawing by Degas shows four young dancers backstage at the Paris Opera House.

Green and Yellow Dancers
By Edgar Degas, drawn between 1870 and 1900

Degas made lots of paintings of ballerinas, opera singers and ordinary people in Paris. At the time, Paris was one of the biggest, most exciting cities in the world, and Degas recorded it in his paintings.

Degas wasn't just a painter – he also experimented with photography, which had recently been invented.

Renoir made lots of paintings of modern Paris, such as this view of a busy city street in the rain.

The Umbrellas
By Pierre-Auguste Renoir, painted in about 1881-6

Renoir originally gave this woman a frilly dress, but painted over it in a new style a few years later.

This sunny painting shows the French town of Marly, which had been flooded. The artist rowed around the town to make sketches for the painting.

Boat in the Flood at Port Marly
By Alfred Sisley, painted in 1876

Renoir loved painting clothes, and thought of an inventive way to study the latest fashions. He persuaded his brother to stop well-dressed people in the street and ask them silly questions, while he secretly sketched their outfits.

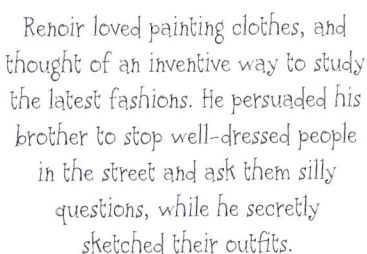

Excuse me, Madam, but where are we? What time is it? Who are you?

The little girl wears the frilly clothes that were fashionable when Renoir began the picture.

23

BRIGHT AND BOLD

The Impressionists inspired the artists who came after them to use brighter, sunnier colours. But the new artists also invented different ways of painting, and found new subjects to paint.

These yellow sunflowers were painted by Dutch artist, Vincent van Gogh, for his friend Gauguin. For van Gogh, yellow was the colour of happiness and friendship.

Van Gogh sometimes squeezed paint straight from his tubes onto the canvas.

SUNFLOWERS
By Vincent van Gogh, painted in 1888

Up close, you can see van Gogh's brushstrokes. Notice how thick the paint is.

In the 1880s, Japanese prints became very fashionable in Europe. Both van Gogh and Gauguin collected them.

This painting shows two women on the island of Tahiti, in the South Pacific. The artist, Gauguin, spent most of his life in France, but then moved to Tahiti, hoping to find a simpler, more peaceful way of life there.

Inspired by Japanese prints, Gauguin used flat shapes and strong outlines in his paintings. He also used lots of bold, unusual colours - notice the bright blue shadows behind the women.

THE SUIJIN WOODS AND MASSAKI ON THE SUMIDA RIVER
By Utagawa Hiroshige, designed in 1856

"I shut my eyes in order to see."
Gauguin

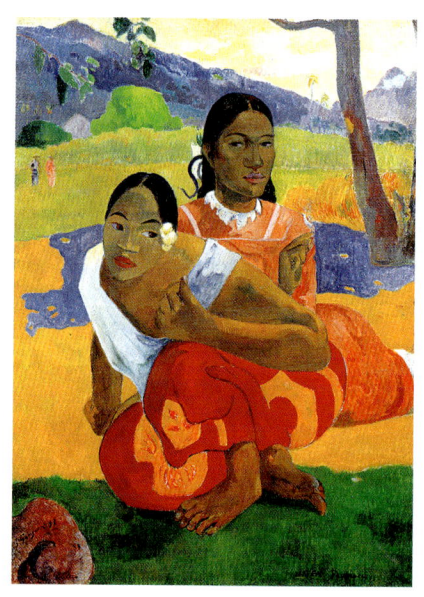

WHEN WILL YOU MARRY?
By Paul Gauguin, painted in 1892

From 1880

In real life, this painting of people by a river is 3 metres (10 feet) long. At the time, it was very unusual for an artist to paint ordinary people on such a grand scale. Paintings this big usually showed kings or queens.

Bathers at Asnières
By Georges Seurat, painted in 1884

Seurat was inspired by ancient Egyptian art, which always showed people from the side.

The people's clothes show they are workers, maybe from the factories in the background.

Seurat makes the river look like a peaceful place to relax – but in real life, it was very noisy and the water smelled of rotten eggs.

Artist Rousseau claimed to have painted this picture after going to the jungle with the French army...

...but he never actually left France. He probably sketched this tiger at the zoo.

Surprised!
By Henri Rousseau, painted in 1891

Rousseau probably based his jungle plants on house plants and specimens he'd seen at a botanical garden.

Toulouse-Lautrec made bold, colourful prints of night life in Paris. He designed this poster to advertise a friend's cabaret show. But his posters were so popular, they were often stolen as soon as they were put up.

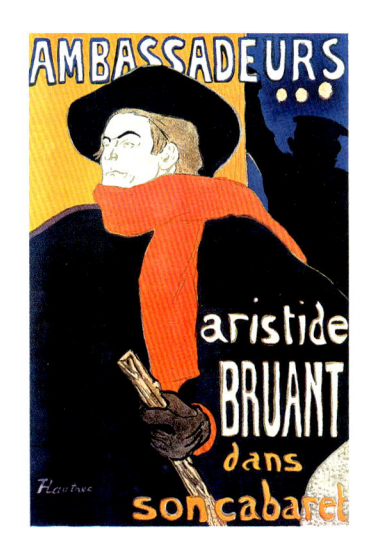

Ambassadeurs: Aristide Bruant
By Henri de Toulouse-Lautrec, printed in 1892

WILD AND FREE

From 1905

The bright, colourful paintings of van Gogh and Gauguin inspired the next generation of painters to use even wilder, brighter colours.

When this painting was first shown, it was in a show held by a group of artists who all liked using unusual colours. One critic was so shocked by their paintings, he gave them the nickname 'wild beasts'.

Henri Matisse added lots of bright, strange colours to this portrait of his wife. He used green, orange, pink, brown, yellow and blue – just to paint her face.

WOMAN WITH A HAT
By Henri Matisse, painted in 1905

Wild beasts!

Notice the strange colours in this port scene by Matisse's friend, André Derain – the distant hills are painted green, blue, pink and red.

As well as painting pictures, Derain and Matisse also designed brightly coloured costumes and sets for ballets.

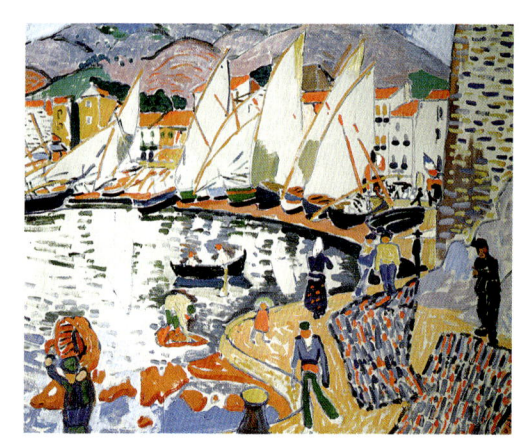

DRYING THE SAILS
By André Derain, painted in 1905

The painter who made this bright self-portrait thought that artists shouldn't have to follow any rules at all. They shouldn't even have to get dressed. That's why he painted himself in his dressing gown.

AN ARTIST AND HIS MODEL
By Ernst Ludwig Kirchner, painted between 1910 and 1926

26

Breaking ~~Following~~ the Rules

From 1911

At the beginning of the 20th century, some artists made works of art which looked totally different from anything that had ever been made before.

At first, it's hard to tell what is happening in this picture. It's a sort of picture puzzle.

It actually shows a table in a café, but the artist, Picasso, painted the objects from different angles, so everything looks jumbled up. Look closely and see if you can find a candle, a cup, a table and some peas.

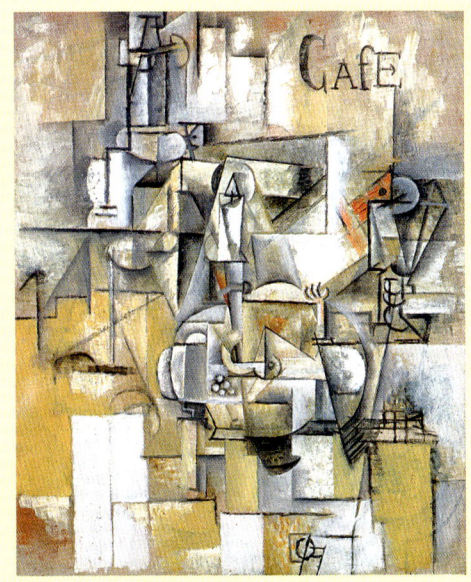

Pigeon with Peas
By Pablo Picasso, painted in 1911

This painting of a horse looks almost as if it has been cut up and put back together again. The artist, Boccioni, loved painting fast moving objects. His jagged style makes it look as if the horse is racing along.

Elasticity
By Umberto Boccioni, painted in 1912

"All children are artists. The trick is to remain one when you grow up."
Picasso

Slanting lines add to the feeling of speed.

Marcel Duchamp was a young artist during the First World War, when millions of people died. Duchamp thought the world had gone mad, so mad he couldn't respect anything any more – not even great artists like Leonardo da Vinci.

That's why Duchamp added a moustache and a beard to this reproduction of Leonardo da Vinci's famous painting, the *Mona Lisa*.

Duchamp also attached a bicycle wheel to a stool, and called it 'art'.

L.H.O.O.Q.
By Marcel Duchamp, created in 1919

From 1918

SHAPES AND DREAMS

After the First World War, the world changed, and art did too. Some artists became more interested in creating patterns than in painting pictures of real life. Other artists produced strange imaginary scenes.

Kandinsky was one of the first artists to paint pictures that didn't show real-life scenes. Instead, he painted interesting shapes and colours. This became known as 'abstract art'.

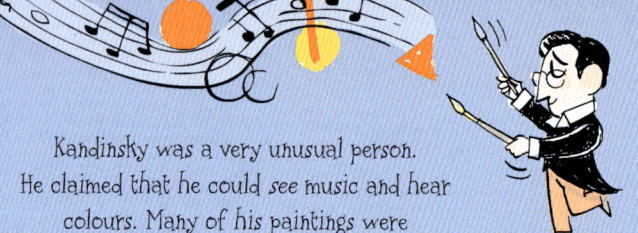

Kandinsky was a very unusual person. He claimed that he could *see* music and hear colours. Many of his paintings were inspired by music.

IN BLUE (IM BLAU, R. 731)
By Wassily Kandinsky, painted in 1925

This bizarre-looking painting was made by Spanish artist, Salvador Dalí. Dalí wanted his works of art to look like dreams. In this scene, he has imagined sleep as a monstrous head.

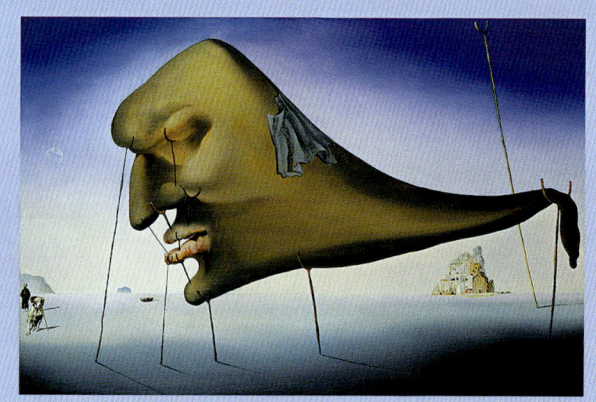

Dalí also made sculptures by putting surprising objects together. One of his most famous sculptures was a telephone with a lobster on top.

SLEEP
By Salvador Dalí, painted in 1937

Spanish artist Joan Miró was inspired by ancient cave paintings. He wanted his art to be simple and magical, like them. This dream-like painting uses very simplified figures. Look closely – can you find a moon and stars, and more shapes that might be a woman and a bird?

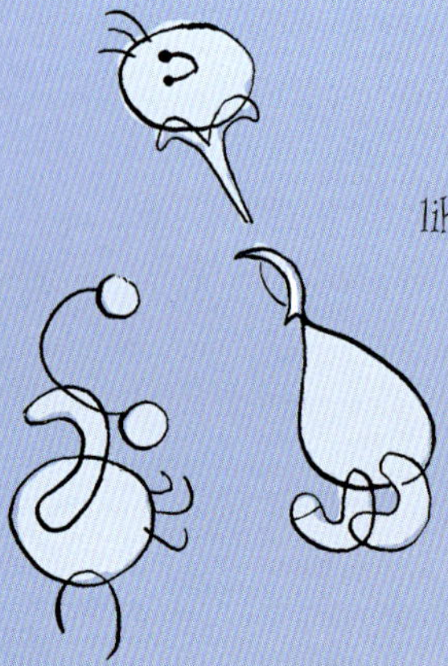

WOMAN AND BIRD IN THE MOONLIGHT
by Joan Miró, painted in 1949

1950–today

THINK AGAIN

Since the 1950s, artists have invented lots of new styles. Today, artists don't just paint pictures or make sculptures, they create art in all sorts of different ways. Art is changing all the time, and it's impossible to predict what artists will do next.

American artist Jackson Pollock made this painting by laying an enormous canvas flat on the floor, and then dripping paint all over it.

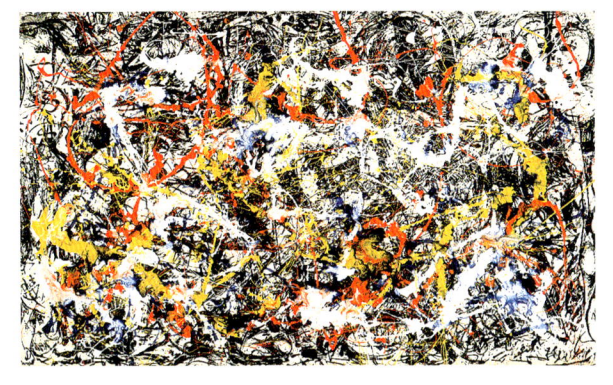

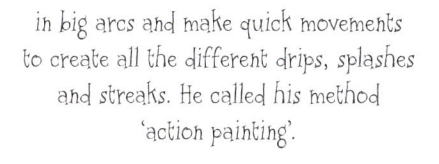

Pollock would move his brush in big arcs and make quick movements to create all the different drips, splashes and streaks. He called his method 'action painting'.

CONVERGENCE
By Jackson Pollock, painted in 1952

In the 1960s, lots of artists made art using images from magazines, newspapers and television.

This enormous painting, by American artist Roy Lichtenstein, was inspired by a comic strip.

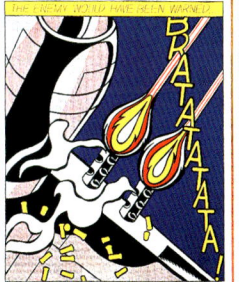

AS I OPENED FIRE
By Roy Lichtenstein, painted in 1964

French-American artist Louise Bourgeois created a gigantic metal spider titled *Maman*, which means 'mummy' in French. The viewer can walk underneath and look up at it, like a small child looking up to its mother.

Some artists make art for a particular space. This is known as 'installation art'. One installation by Anish Kapoor featured a cannon complete with red wax bombs that exploded against the wall opposite.

SHOOTING INTO THE CORNER
By Anish Kapoor, made in 2008–9

MAMAN
By Louise Bourgeois, made in 1999

TIMELINE

Around 17,000 years ago — People in lots of different parts of the world paint on the walls of caves.

2,500 years ago — Greek artists are making lifelike paintings and sculptures. This ancient Greek cup dates from 2,500 years ago.

800s — Christian monks are producing handmade books.

1600s — Dutch artists make paintings of ordinary objects, called 'still lifes'.

1800s — Photography is invented in 1830.

Thomas Gainsborough paints *Mr and Mrs William Hallett (The Morning Walk)* in 1785.

Between 1835-40, J.M.W. Turner paints *Margate (?) from the Sea*.

In 1841, metal paint tubes are invented, and more artists start painting outside.

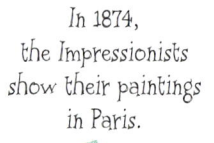

1800s — In 1874, the Impressionists show their paintings in Paris.

In 1888, Vincent van Gogh paints *Sunflowers*.

1910s — Artist Marcel Duchamp takes everyday objects, such as a bicycle wheel, and exhibits them as art.

1920s — Kandinsky is one of the first artists to paint pictures that don't show real-life scenes. This becomes known as 'abstract art'.

1930s — Surrealist artists such as Salvador Dalí create bizarre, dreamlike artworks.

1960s

30

In 1333, Simone Martini and Lippo Memmi paint *The Annunciation*.

Artists in the Netherlands are using oil paints.

Artists in Italy are inspired by ancient Greek and Roman art.

Artists in Europe use rich materials to make religious paintings.

In 1434, Jan van Eyck paints *The Arnolfini Portrait*.

1400s

Around 1438-40, Italian artist Paolo Uccello paints *The Battle of San Romano*.

During the 16th century, many wealthy people have their portraits painted.

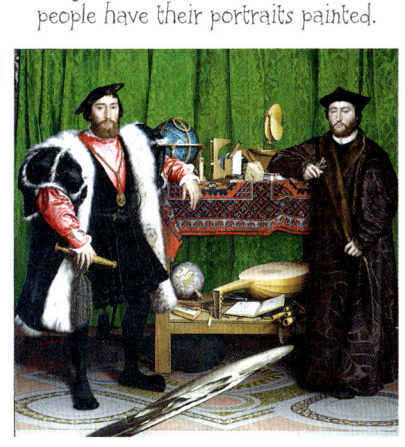

1500s

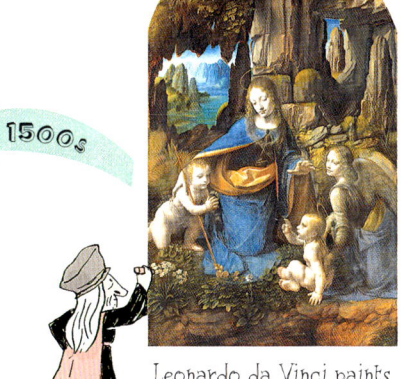

Leonardo da Vinci paints *The Virgin of the Rocks* in about 1491-1508.

1450s

Artists start to study living and dead bodies, to make their pictures more realistic.

In 1533, Hans Holbein paints *The Ambassadors*.

1980s and 90s

Some artists make works for particular places. These are called 'installations'.

2000s

David Hockney makes collages with polaroids.

Many artists use film and photography to make art.

1970s

Many artists are inspired by adverts and pop music to create Pop art.

Anish Kapoor creates *Shooting Into The Corner*, an installation with red wax bombs, in 2008-9.

31

INDEX

3rd of May 1808 in Madrid: the Executions on Principe Pio Hill, The, 19
Adoration of the Magi, 6
Ambassadeurs: Aristide Bruant, 25
Ambassadors, The, 12, 31
Annunciation, The, 5, 8
Arcimboldo, Giuseppe, 12
Arnolfini Portrait, The, 7, 31
Artist and his Model, An 26
As I Opened Fire, 29
At the Theatre, 22
Bacchus and Ariadne, 11
Bathers at Asnières, 25
Battle of San Romano, The, 9, 31
Belshazzar's Feast, 13
Birth of Venus, The, 8
Bison, 2
Boat in the Flood at Port Marly, 23
Boccioni, Umberto, 27
Bosschaert, Ambrosius (the Elder), 15
Botticelli, Sandro, 8
Bourgeois, Louise, 29
Boy Bitten by a Lizard, 13
Bruegel, Pieter (the Elder), 14
Burning of Babylon, The, 4
Caravaggio, 13
Cassatt, Mary, 22
Cézanne, Paul, 22
Chardin, Jean-Siméon, 18
Château de Médan, The, 22
Children's Games, 14
Christ Enthroned, 4
Claude, 18
Constable, John, 20
Convergence, 29
Cornfield, The, 20
Cup featuring Athletes, 3
da Fabriano, Gentile, 6
Dalí, Salvador, 28, 30
David, Jacques-Louis, 19
da Vinci, Leonardo, 11, 31
Degas, Edgar, 23
Delacroix, Eugène, 19
del Mazo, Juan Bautista Martínez, 12
Derain, André, 26
di Cosimo, Piero, 9
Death and the Miser, 7
Dolphin Frescoes, 3
Drying the Sails, 26
Duchamp, Marcel, 27, 30

Effects of Intemperance, The, 14
Elasticity, 27
Empress Theodora, 5
Flaming June, 21
Frederic, Lord Leighton, 21
Friedrich, Caspar David, 20
Gainsborough, Thomas, 16, 30
Gaugin, Paul, 24
Goya, Francisco de, 16, 19
Green and Yellow Dancers, 23
Head of a Horse of Selene, 3
Hiroshige, Utagawa, 24
Hockney, David, 31
Holbein, Hans (the Younger), 12, 31
Horse, 2
House of Cards, The, 18
In Blue, 28
Ingres, Jean-Auguste-Dominique, 18
January, 6
Judith and Maidservant with the Head of Holofernes, 13
Kandinsky, Wassily, 28, 30
Kapoor, Anish, 29, 31
Kirchner, Ernst Ludwig, 26
Lady of Shalott, 21
L.H.O.O.Q., 27
Liberty Leading the People, 19
Lichtenstein, Roy, 29
Limbourg Brothers, 6
Lippi, Fra Filippo, 8
Madame de Pompadour, 17
Madonna and Child, 5
Maman, 29
Manuel Osorio Manrique de Zuñiga, 16
Margate (?) from the Sea, 20, 30
Marie Antoinette, Queen of France, 17
Martini, Simone, 5, 31
Matisse, Henri, 26
Memmi, Lippo, 5, 31
Michelangelo, 10
Miró, Joan, 28
Monet, Claude-Oscar, 22
Moreau, Gustave, 21
Mr and Mrs William Hallett (The Morning Walk), 16, 30
Napoleon Crossing the Alps, 19
Ornamental Pool from the Tomb of Nebamun, 2
Perseus Frees Andromeda, 9
Petrus, 4

Picasso, Pablo, 27
Pierrot, formerly known as Gilles, 16
Pigeon with Peas, 27
Pollock, Jackson, 29
Portrait of a Lady, 7
Portrait of Rudolph II, 12
Portrait of the Infanta Margarita in a Pink Dress, 12
Raphael, 11
Rembrandt, 13
Rousseau, Henri, 25
St. George and the Dragon, 21
Scene on the Ice near a Town, A, 15
Scenes from the Sistine Chapel Ceiling, 10
Seaport with the Embarkation of the Queen of Sheba, 18
Seurat, Georges, 25
Shooting into the Corner, 29, 31
Sign for a Thermopolium, 3
Sleep, 28
Steen, Jan, 14
Still Life of Flowers in a Wan-Li Vase, A, 15
St. George Struggling with the Dragon, 11
Study for an Odalisque, 18
Sujin Woods and Massaki on the Sumida River, The, 24
Sunflowers, 24, 30
Surprised!, 25
Swing, The, 17
Titian, 11
Toulouse-Lautrec, Henri de, 25
Turner, J.M.W., 20, 30
Uccello, Paolo, 9, 31
Umbrellas, The, 23
van der Weyden, Rogier, 7
van Eyck, Jan, 7, 31
van Gogh, Vincent, 24, 30
Vigée Le Brun, Elisabeth Louise, 17
Virgin of the Rocks, The, 11, 31
Visigoth, 4
Wanderer Above the Sea of Fog, 20
Waterhouse, John William, 21
Water-Lily Pond, The, 22
Watteau, Jean-Antoine, 16
When will you marry?, 24
Woman and Bird in the Moonlight, 28
Woman with a Hat, 26
Young Woman Seated at a Virginal, A, 14

USBORNE QUICKLINKS

See lots more masterpieces and tour art galleries online by going to the Usborne Quicklinks website at www.usborne.com/quicklinks and typing the keywords 'story of art'. Please read our internet safety guidelines at the Usborne Quicklinks website.

ACKNOWLEDGEMENTS

Pages 2-3: Horse cave painting from Lascaux © Bettmann/CORBIS, Rock painting of Bison © Bridgeman Art Library; Garden of a private estate, part of the wall painting from the Tomb of Nebamun © British Museum, London, UK/The Bridgeman Art Library; Dolphin fresco from the Palace of Knossos © Photo Spectrum/Heritage Images/Scala, Florence; Sphinx surrounded by athletes, poultry, wild and mythical animals © Photo Scala, Florence/BPK, Bildagentur fuer Kunst, Kultur und Geschichte, Berlin; Ancient Greek head of a horse of Selene © Steven Vidler/Eurasia Press/Corbis; Sign for the thermopolium (taverna) depicting a phoenix Roman/Antiquarium, Pompeii, Italy/Giraudon/The Bridgeman Art Library. Pages 4-5: Christ Enthroned from the Book of Kells © Heritage Images/Corbis; Visigoth from 'Apocalypse de Silos' © White Images/Scala, Florence; Commentary on the Apocalypse of Beatus de Liebana: The Burning of Babylon/Photo Pierpont Morgan Library/Art Resource/Scala, Florence; The Annunciation with two saints by Simone Martini and Lippo Memmi © Summerfield Press/Corbis; Vladimir Madonna by Rublev, Andrei (c.1370-1430) (circle of)/State Russian Museum, St. Petersburg, Russia/The Bridgeman Art Library; Empress Theodora © Byzantine School, (6th century)/San Vitale, Ravenna, Italy/Giraudon/The Bridgeman Art Library. Pages 6-7: The Adoration of the Magi by Gentile da Fabriano © Summerfield Press/Corbis; January from The Very Rich Hours of the Duke of Berry © White Images/Scala, Florence; The Arnolfini Portrait by Jan van Eyck © The National Gallery, London; Portrait of a Lady, Workshop of Rogier van der Weyden © The Print Collector/Corbis; Death and the Miser by Hieronymus Bosch © The Art Gallery Collection/Alamy. Pages 8-9: The Annunciation by Fra Filippo Lippi © The National Gallery, London; The Birth of Venus by Sandro Botticelli © The Gallery Collection/Corbis; The Battle of San Romano by Paulo Uccello © The National Gallery, London; Perseus frees Andromeda by Piero di Cosimo © The Art Archive/Alamy. Pages 10-11: Sistine Chapel Ceiling by Michelangelo © Vatican Museums & Galleries, Vatican City/Bridgeman Art Library; The Virgin of the Rocks by Leonardo da Vinci © The National Gallery, London; Bacchus and Ariadne by Titian © The National Gallery, London; St. George struggling with the Dragon by Raphael © The Art Gallery Collection /Alamy. Pages 12-13: The Ambassadors by Hans Holbein the Younger © The National Gallery, London; Portrait of Rudolf II by Giuseppi Arcimboldo © The Art Archive/Alamy; Portrait of The Infanta Margarita of Austria, by Juan Bautista Martinez del Mazo © Prado, Madrid, Spain/The Bridgeman Art Library; Boy bitten by a Lizard by Caravaggio © The National Gallery, London; Belshazzar's Feast by Rembrandt © The National Gallery, London; Judith and Maidservant with the Head of Holofernes © Detroit Institute of Arts, USA/ Gift of Mr Leslie H. Green/The Bridgeman Art Library. Pages 14-15: Children's games by Pieter Bruegel the Elder © Ali Meyer/Corbis; The Effects of Intemperance by Jan Steen © The National Gallery, London; A Young Woman Seated at a Virginal by Johannes Vermeer © The National Gallery, London; A Still Life of Flowers in a Wan-Li Vase by Ambrosius Bosschaert the Elder © The National Gallery, London; A Scene on the Ice near a Town by Hendrick Avercamp © The National Gallery, London. Pages 16-17: Mr and Mrs William Hallett (the Morning Walk) by Thomas Gainsborough © The National Gallery, London; Pierrot, formerly known as Gilles by Jean-Antoine Watteau © Alfredo Dagli Orti/The Art Archive/Corbis; Manuel Osorio Manrique de Zuniga by Francisco de Goya © Tomas Abad/Alamy; Madame de Pompadour by François Boucher © Wallace Collection, London, UK/The Bridgeman Art Library; The Swing by Jean-Honoré Fragonard © Lebrecht Music and Arts Photo Library/Alamy. By kind permission of the Trustees of the Wallace Collection, London; Marie Antoinette, Queen of France, 1779, by Elisabeth Vigée-Lebrun/Chateau de Versailles, France/The Bridgeman Art Library. Pages 18-19: Seaport with the Embarkation of the Queen of Sheba by Claude © The National Gallery, London; Study for an Odalisque by Jean-Auguste-Dominique Ingres © The Gallery Collection/Corbis; The House of Cards by Jean-Siméon Chardin © The National Gallery, London; Napoleon Crossing the Alps by Jacques-Louis David © The Art Archive/Musée du Château de Versailles/Collection Dagli Orti; Liberty Leading the People by Eugène Delacroix © The Art Gallery Collection/Alamy; The 3rd of May 1808 in Madrid: the executions on Principe Pio Hill by Francisco de Goya © The Gallery Collection/Corbis; Pages 20-21: Margate (?) from the Sea by J.M.W. Turner © The National Gallery, London; The Cornfield by John Constable © The National Gallery, London; Wanderer Above The Sea of Fog by Caspar David Friedrich © The Art Archive/Kunsthalle Hamburg/Superstock; Saint George and the Dragon by Gustave Moreau © The National Gallery, London; Flaming June by Lord Frederic Leighton © Corbis; The Lady of Shalott by John William Waterhouse © Photo Art Media/Heritage Images/Scala, Florence. Pages 22-23: The Water-Lily Pond by Claude-Oscar Monet © The National Gallery, London; The Château de Médan by Paul Cézanne/Burrell Collection, Glasgow, Scotland/© Culture and Sport Glasgow (Museums)/The Bridgeman Art Library; At the Theater by Mary Cassatt © The Nelson-Atkins Museum of Art, Kansas City, Missouri. Purchase: acquired through the generosity of an anonymous donor, F77-33. Photo credit: Jamison Miller; Green and Yellow Dancers by Edgar Degas © Christie's Images/Corbis; Boat in the Flood at Port Marly by Alfred Sisley © Masterpics/Alamy; The Umbrellas by Pierre-Auguste Renoir © The National Gallery, London. Pages 24-25: Sunflowers by Vincent van Gogh © The National Gallery, London; The Suigin Woods and Massaki on the Sumida River by Utagawa Hiroshige, presented by Mr and Mrs H Spalding © Ashmolean Museum, University of Oxford, UK/The Bridgeman Art Library; Quand te maries tu? (When will you marry?) by Paul Gauguin/White Images/Scala, Florence; Bathers at Ashières by Georges Seurat © The National Gallery, London; Surprised! by Henri Rousseau © The National Gallery, London; Ambassadeurs: Artistide Bruant by Henri de Toulouse Lautrec © Lordprice Collection/Alamy. Pages 26-27: Henri Matisse, Femme au chapeau (Woman with a Hat), 1905 oil on canvas; 31 3/4 in. x 23 1/2 in. (80.65 cm x 59.69 cm); San Francisco Museum of Modern Art, San Francisco Museum of Modern Art, Bequest of Elise S. Haas; © Succession H. Matisse/ DACS 2017, Photo credit: Ben Blackwell; Drying the Sails by André Derain © ADAGP, Paris and DACS, London 2017, photo credit © Pushkin Museum, Moscow, Russia, The Bridgeman Art Library; An artist and his model by Ernst Ludwig Kirchner © The Gallery Collection/Corbis; Pigeon with Peas by Pablo Picasso © Succession Picasso/DACS, London 2017, photo credit: © The Gallery Collection/Corbis; Elasticity by Umberto Boccioni/Pinacoteca di Brera, Milan, Italy/The Bridgeman Art Library; L.H.O.O.Q by Marcel Duchamp © Association Marcel Duchamp/ADAGP, Paris and DACS, London 2017, photo credit: © Burstein Collection/Corbis/. Pages 28-29: Im Blau (In Blue), 1925 (R. 731) by Wassily Kandinsky © Alinari Archives/CORBIS; Sleep by Salvador Dalí © Salvador Dalí, Fundació Gala-Salvador Dalí, DACS, 2017, photo credit © Christie's Images/CORBIS; Woman and Bird in the Moonlight by Joan Miró © Successió Miró/ADAGP, Paris and DACS, London 2017, photo credit: © The Art Archive/Tate Gallery London; Convergence by Jackson Pollock © The Pollock-Krasner Foundation ARS, NY and DACS, London 2017, photo credit: Albright-Knox Art Gallery/Corbis; As I Opened Fire by Roy Lichtenstein © The Estate of Roy Lichtenstein/DACS 2017, photo credit: © DeAgostini/SuperStock; Maman by Louise Bourgeois at Kunstalle, Hamburg 2012 © The Easton Foundation/VAGA New York/DACS, London 2017, photo credit © Christian Ohde/Mc Photo/Ullstein bild via Getty Images; Shooting into the corner by Anish Kapoor © Anish Kapoor. All Rights Reserved, DACS 2017. Page 30-31: Sphinx surrounded by athletes, poultry, wild and mythical animals: credit as on pages 2-3; Mr and Mrs William Hallett (The Morning Walk): credit as on pages 16-17; The Annunciation by Simone Martini and Lippo Memmi: credit as on pages 4-5, Margate (?) from the Sea: credit as on pages 20-21; Sunflowers by Vincent van Gogh: credit as on pages 24-25; The Arnolfini Portrait by Jan van Eyck: credit as on pages 6-7; The Battle of San Romano by Paulo Uccello: credit as on pages 8-9; The Ambassadors by Hans Holbein the Younger: credit as on pages 12-13; Shooting in the Corner by Anish Kapoor: credit as on pages 28-29. Cover: Surprised! by Henri Rousseau © The National Gallery, London; The Arnolfini Portrait by Jan van Eyck © The National Gallery, London; Detail from The Birth of Venus by Sandro Botticelli © The Gallery Collection/Corbis. Bathers at Ashières by Georges Seurat © The National Gallery, London. Back cover: The Water-Lily Pond by Claude-Oscar Monet © The National Gallery, London.

This edition first published in 2018 by Usborne Publishing Ltd., Usborne House, 83-85 Saffron Hill, London EC1N 8RT, England. www.usborne.com Copyright © 2018, 2012 Usborne Publishing Ltd. All rights reserved. No part of this publication may be reproduced, stored in a retrieval system or transmitted in any form or by any means, electronic, mechanical, photocopying, recording or otherwise, without the prior permission of the publisher. The name Usborne and the devices are Trade Marks of Usborne Publishing Ltd. UKE.